DATE DUE

APR 20		
MAY 04		
NOV 08		
APR 16		
JAN 03		
OCT 08 2008		
DEC 01 2008		

HIGHSMITH #45230

D1055375

MARK MCGWIRE

HOME-RUN KING

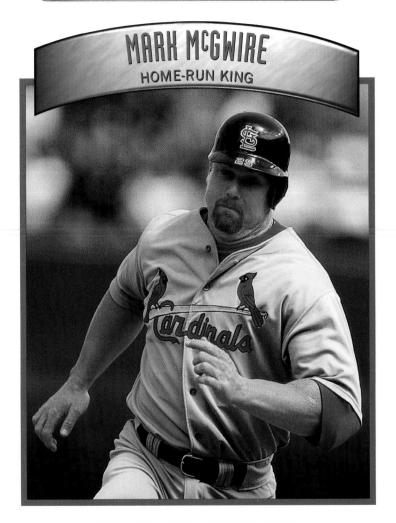

BY MARK STEWART

 Children's Press®

A Division of Grolier Publishing
New York London Hong Kong Sydney
Danbury, Connecticut

Photo Credits

Photographs ©: AllSport USA: 32, 36 (Brian Bahr), 23, 45 left (Otto Greule), 20 (Greule Jr.), 40 (Jacobsohn), 42 top, 39 (Vincent Laforet); AP/Wide World Photos: 26 top; Archive Photos: 42 bottom (Reuters/Gary Hershorn), 41, 45 right (Sporting News); Corbis-Bettmann: 25 (UPI); John Klein: 6, 46, 47; Mel Bailey: 15, 17 top, 19, 44 right; SportsChrome East/West: 11 (Jeff Carlick), 12 (Brian Drake), 3, 33, 37 (Rob Tringali Jr.), 30 (Ron Wyatt), 26 bottom, 29; Tom DiPace: cover; USC Sports Information, L.A., CA: 14, 17 bottom, 44 left.

Visit Children's Press on the Internet at:
http://publishing.grolier.com

Library of Congress Cataloging-in-Publication Data

Stewart, Mark.
    Mark McGwire: home-run king / by Mark Stewart.
        p. cm. — (Sports stars)
        Includes index.
        Summary: Presents a biography of the St. Louis Cardinal slugger who broke Roger Maris' single-season home run record in 1998.
        ISBN 0-516-21612-0 (lib. bdg.)   0-516-26512-1 (pbk.)
        1. McGwire, Mark, 1963– —Juvenile literature.
    2. Baseball players—United States—Biography—Juvenile literature. [1. McGwire, Mark, 1963– . 2. Baseball players.]
    I. Title. II. Series.
GV865.M396S84   1999
796.357'092—dc21
[B]   98-48386
                                            CIP
                                          AC

★ CONTENTS ★

★ 1 ★

"BIG MAC"

The pitcher finishes his warm-ups, and the catcher fires the ball around the infield to start a new inning. The noise in the stadium begins to build, reaching an earsplitting level as Mark McGwire sets himself in the batter's box. A game of cat-and-mouse follows, with pitches darting in and out of the strike zone and the Cardinals' superstar waiting patiently for a ball he can drive. With the count full and the ballpark buzzing, the pitcher feels a surge of confidence; he decides to challenge Mark with a heater over the inside corner. But as soon as he releases the ball, he wants it back. He can see Mark's eyes open wide—this is the pitch he was waiting for. Massive forearms whip the bat toward the plate, and superstrong wrists snap it through the hitting zone. *Crack!* In an instant, all eyes are fixed on the left fielder, who stands motionless as the ball sails over his head. The crowd goes berserk as the St. Louis slugger rounds the bases. His 500-foot homer is something other players can only dream about. For Mark, it's just another day at the office.

★ 2 ★

SPORTS ZONE

John and Ginger McGwire's house, in the quiet Los Angeles suburb of Claremont, was anything but quiet. Thanks to their big, athletic sons, it served as the neighborhood sports palace. On any given day, there might be a football game in the backyard, a soccer game in the front yard, a baseball game out in the cul-de-sac, a basketball game in the driveway, or a wrestling match spilling from one room into another.

Mark was the second of five sons born to the McGwires. The oldest brother, Mike, specialized in soccer and golf, as did the third brother, Bobby. Dan, who grew to be the tallest of the McGwires, was a star quarterback. Jay, the youngest, might have been the best athlete of all. As a kid, Mark was mostly interested in the games his older brother played. At five, he was caddying for his dad and playing for a peewee soccer team. Baseball did not enter his life until he turned eight.

Mark had hacked around in neighborhood baseball games, but before he and a friend joined a local youth league, he had never participated in organized baseball. His natural golf stroke helped him become a good hitter, and his strong arm made him an ideal pitcher and shortstop. The same year Mark started playing ball, he was fitted with glasses. His performance improved dramatically, and he became the star of his team.

Mark's parents loved all sports and encouraged their children to play whatever they liked. But as Mark was ready to join the Claremont Little League, they got nervous. They had heard that some of the parents who attended games yelled at their kids from the stands and insulted boys on other teams. Mark was a sensitive, gentle child, and his parents feared

Mark uses contact lenses today. As a Little Leaguer he wore glasses.

he might be over-whelmed. The McGwires kept him out of Little League until they were sure he could handle the pressure. Finally, at the age of 10, Mark became a Little Leaguer. That season he batted fourth, played shortstop, and pitched. His team, the Athletics, won every game he started on the mound. In his first at bat, he blasted a home run. Unfortunately, Mark's parents were out of town and could not attend the game. "When they got back from their trip and pulled into the driveway, I ran out to the car," he laughs. "Without even saying hi, I told them all about that first home run."

Mark's success on the diamond did not convince him that his future was in baseball. When he daydreamed, he thought about being a police officer or a firefighter when he grew up. If he had had to pick a sport at that age, he would have chosen golf. "The thing I liked about golf is that you were the only one to blame when things went wrong," he says.

Mark got more serious about sports after enrolling at Damien High School. That spring he had to choose a sport and devote himself fully to it. He was a great baseball player and a great golfer, so the decision was hard. He went with golf at first and got his handicap down to

four strokes, which is excellent for a boy of 15. But Mark found himself thinking more and more about the sport he had left behind. "I missed baseball," he remembers, "and I went back to it."

Mark does not regret choosing baseball over golf.

★ 3 ★

HIGH MARKS
FOR BASEBALL

In three seasons with the Damien High baseball team, Mark distinguished himself as one of the best prep players in California. In his senior year, he stood 6' 5" and weighed a muscular 200 pounds. When he threw the ball, hitters could barely see it coming; when he hit the ball, it sometimes cleared the outfield fence by 100 feet or more. After graduation, Mark turned down an offer from the Montreal Expos to turn pro. Instead, he accepted a scholarship from the University of Southern California (USC).

Mark's first year in college was a tough one. He pitched well enough, but his hitting was atrocious. He felt he was letting down Coach

Rod Dedeaux. Little did Mark know, the coach could not have been more pleased. He loved the big freshman's work ethic and his intense desire to improve. He could see a star in the making, even if Mark could not. After the season, Dedeaux suggested that Mark join the Alaskan

Mark's intense desire to improve his hitting dates back to his USC days.

summer league. He wanted him to get a couple of months of topflight baseball under his belt, and he also wanted him to play far away from California, where the distractions of home and family would not be present.

In Alaska, Mark was very homesick at first. But by the end of the summer he had blossomed into a patient hitter, and he began to exhibit the qualities of a true team leader. "I was away from home for the first time in my life, with a group of people I didn't know," Mark recalls. "Instead of quitting and going home—which would have been the easy thing to do—I stuck it out. As a result, I gained confidence in myself, and I grew up."

Mark warms up in the Trojan bullpen. His pitching career ended after his second college season.

☆ ☆ ☆

As a sophomore, Mark did a lot more hitting
and a lot less pitching. Soon he was involved in
his first "home run chase," as he closed in on the
USC school record of 17. He blasted the record-
tying round-tripper with a couple of weeks to go,
then added three more home runs to make it 20
for the year. The next target for Mark was the
USC career record for homers, which was 32. He
not only eclipsed that record in his junior year,
but he blasted 32 in one season. He hit them
often, and he hit them far—against Arizona,
Mark smashed one ball that no one ever found!

After that season, things really heated up for
Mark. He was selected by the Oakland Athletics
in the first round of the baseball draft; he
married his girlfriend, Kathy Williamson; and
he was selected to play for Team USA in the
1984 Olympics. It was quite a spring!

Mark returns to
the dugout (top)
after scoring a
run for Team USA.
His 32 home runs
for USC in 1984
(right) established
a new record.

★ 4 ★

RECORD-BREAKING ROOKIE

Mark signed a big contract with the Oakland A's, and after the Olympics he reported for duty with their minor-league team in Modesto, California, where he participated in a few games before the season ended. Playing for Modesto again in 1985, Mark came to the plate 585 times and led the California League with 24 homers and 106 RBIs. That performance earned him a promotion to Class-AA Huntsville, to start the 1986 campaign. He did not last long there, smashing 10 homers in 55 games, and dominating Southern League pitchers. After moving up to the organization's AAA farm team

Few fans realize that Mark spent the entire 1986 season at third base!

in Tacoma, Mark hit 13 more home runs and batted over .300. When the minor-league season ended, he was called up to the majors.

With Oakland, Mark got to play in 18 games at the end of the 1986 season. He had a chance to meet the club's veteran infielders Tony Phillips, Carney Lansford, and Alfredo Griffin. The plan was to install Mark at first base in 1987, so it was good that he got to spend time with them. He also got to reunite with former minor-league teammates Terry Steinbach, Mike Gallego, Walt Weiss, Stan Javier, and José Canseco, who was putting the finishing touches on a great rookie season.

Oakland slugger Jose Canseco. His brilliant 1986 rookie season gave Mark something to shoot for in 1987.

★ ★ ★

The 1987 season began with Canseco in the spotlight. He had hit 33 homers the year before, and many believed he could become the first player ever to hit 40 homers and steal 40 bases in the same year. "José Mania" was out of control—everyone hounded him for his autograph, fans were paying top dollar for his year-old rookie card, and green-and-gold jerseys bearing number 33 sold out as soon as they hit the stores. Meanwhile, A's fans barely noticed the freckle-faced rookie at first base. That was fine with Mark. He played his first few weeks without any pressure or expectations, and he took his time getting adjusted to life in the major leagues.

Pitchers did not know much about Mark, so they challenged him with fastballs. Of course, that was a big mistake. He began pumping balls out of the park and came within a single home run of breaking the record for homers in the month of May. Now everyone knew who Mark McGwire was. And soon fans began talking about a much more important record for the big redhead: home runs for a rookie. Of course, American League pitchers would have some say in the matter. Indeed, they were watching videotapes of Mark and cooking up new ways to get him out.

Mark showed tremendous maturity for a young slugger. He adjusted to enemy hurlers as quickly as they changed their approach to him, and so he kept his power surge going all season long. Suddenly everyone wanted Mark's autograph, and *his* rookie card hit the $20 mark. And just about every kid in the Bay Area was wearing jersey number 25.

When the year was over, Mark had etched his name in the record books. His 49 homers led the league and obliterated the rookie record of 38. He could have had 50 home runs, but he left the team on the season's final day to witness the birth of his son, Matthew.

Mark follows through on his big swing. He clubbed 49 homers in 1987 to break the rookie record.

★ 5 ★

HIGHS AND LOWS

Some athletes thrive on fame. Others, like young Mark McGwire, get overwhelmed by it. When he returned for the 1988 season, he discovered that the pressure had been cranked up a notch. The A's were no longer a young, up-and-coming club. They were expected to win the pennant, and Mark was expected to improve on his historic rookie season. Off the field, Mark could not go anywhere without being mobbed. His life was no longer his own, and that made him angry. The stress ate away at him, and he and Kathy grew farther apart as the season wore on.

On paper, Mark had a decent year. Despite getting few good pitches to hit, he managed 32 home runs. The A's won the AL Western Division crown by 13 games and beat the Red Sox in the playoffs, earning Mark and his teammates a trip to the World Series. Just before the series, however, Mark and Kathy's marriage ended.

Fed up with her husband's behavior, she took Matthew and left. Mark kicks himself to this day. "Kathy and I never talked about things," he says. "I didn't know how to communicate then . . . I just closed it off."

Kathy and Mark share a rare moment of peace outside their California home.

Jose and Mark's famous "Bash Brothers" poster is highly prized by collectors.

Mark ponders his problems in the Oakland dugout. The 1991 season was a disaster for him.

Mark had good seasons at the plate in 1989 and 1990, and in 1990 he won a Gold Glove for his excellent fielding. The A's, meanwhile, were being hailed as a "dynasty." Led by Mark and José Canseco (now known as the "Bash Brothers"), they swept the San Francisco Giants to win the 1989 World Series and repeated as American League champs in 1990. But the success of the team did not bring Mark much joy. He missed his family, and baseball was beginning to wear him down.

During the 1991 season, Mark neglected his training and stopped making the adjustments that enabled him to stay ahead of the pitchers. Consequently, his average plummeted to .201. He actually asked manager Tony La Russa to bench him at the end of the year because he could not bear the thought of finishing below .200. Mark decided he would rather retire than go through another year like 1991.

On the long drive back home after the season, he thought about his options. That is when things finally became clear to him. "I thought about how much I really loved the game and just decided that there wasn't any room for pouting or complaining, or anything but doing my best," he says.

Mark started working out his problems with a professional counselor, then began to rebuild his body. For that, he turned to his youngest brother, Jay. An eye injury in high school had ended Jay's chances at a pro football career, so he'd turned to body building and weight lifting, hoping to become a personal trainer. His first big client was Mark. The two brothers trained hard all winter, focusing on the parts of Mark's body that wore down fastest during the season. Mark also used special exercises and took nutritional supplements to bulk up his arms and shoulders, so that he could switch to a shorter swing without sacrificing power.

With a sound mind and a rock-solid body, Mark returned to form in 1992, victimizing AL pitchers for 42 home runs and leading the league with a .585 slugging average. Best of all, he brought the A's back to the top of the heap, as they reclaimed the division title. Unfortunately, just when

Mark uses the one-handed follow-through that he learned while waiting for his injuries to heal.

Mark seemed to have it all working again, he was struck by a series of painful injuries. During the 1993 and 1994 seasons, a sore back and heel limited him to just 74 games.

Rather than sulking, the "new" Mark McGwire made the best of a bad situation. Every day, he came to the ballpark determined to learn something new about hitting. One thing he

Mark watches his teammates do battle on the field. Injuries in 1993 and 1994 kept him on the bench for all but 74 games.

discovered was that he was strong enough to use a one-handed follow-through. This would enable him to wait a fraction of a second longer before committing himself to a swing. Also, Mark made up his mind that if pitchers refused to give him a pitch to hit, he simply would not swing. That would force them to throw strikes.

50–50

Mark's new approach to hitting worked wonders. In 1995, he slugged 39 home runs in 104 games and his slugging percentage skyrocketed to .685. In 1996, he managed to stay healthy for 130 games and batted a career-high .312. He also led the majors with 52 home runs and a .730 slugging average, which ranks among the highest marks in history. The Oakland fans took great pride in his numbers, but Mark's satisfaction was dampened by the fact that the A's had fallen on hard times. The franchise was about to enter a long rebuilding phase, and Mark understood that the A's could not afford his salary. He knew his time in Oakland would likely come to an end in 1997.

Until a deal was made, however, Mark decided
to continue where he had left off in 1996. He took
aim at the all-time, single-season record of 61
home runs, which was set by New York Yankees
outfielder Roger Maris in 1961. He was joined
in this quest by Ken Griffey, Jr. of the Seattle
Mariners, who matched Mark homer-for-homer
right through the 1997 season.

At the All-Star break, Mark had 31 home
runs and Griffey had 30, keeping pace with the
immortals. But then Griffey went homerless for
nearly three weeks, and Mark hit just three more

during July.
These slumps
appeared to
put the record
out of reach

**Mark and Ken
Griffey, Jr. chat
during the 1998
All-Star Game.**

Mark watches the ball soar toward the stands. He got hot after joining the Cardinals in 1997 and finished the year with 58 home runs.

for both sluggers. In the meantime, the A's were fielding offers for Mark. The best one came from the power-starved St. Louis Cardinals, who offered Oakland a pair of young relievers. The deal was made official on July 31, and Mark moved over to the National League.

Typically, a hitter changing leagues is at a disadvantage, because he does not know the pitchers. But in a few days, Mark got into a groove that lasted the rest of the year. On Sept. 17, he hit his 20th home run for St. Louis, becoming the first player in baseball history to hit 20 homers for two teams in the same season. Mark finished the year with 58 home runs. He was three short of the Maris record, but joined Hall of Famer Babe Ruth as the only other player to top 50 homers in back-to-back seasons.

★ 7 ★

UNSTOPPABLE

The 1998 season held much promise for those who wished to see the old home-run record fall. The major leagues had added two brand-new teams, the Arizona Diamondbacks and Tampa Bay Devil Rays. This meant there would be a lot of inexperienced pitchers facing veteran sluggers such as Mark, and that would surely translate into more home runs—perhaps enough for someone to reach 61.

Mark began the year with a bang. He hit a grand slam in his very first at bat and homered in each of the next three contests. By the end of April, he added seven more. As many predicted, 1998 was indeed shaping up to be a big year for

**Mark and Sammy Sosa exchange greetings after the Cubs'
star reaches first base.**

home runs. Vinny Castilla of the Rockies, Greg
Vaughn of the Padres, and Ken Griffey, Jr. kept
pace with Mark right through the spring. In
June, Sammy Sosa of the Cubs joined the party,
slamming a record 20 round-trippers during
the month.

For his part, Mark seemed to hit the ball hard
every time up. After a while, sights that would
have seemed silly in the past became common-
place. Mark's third-base coach, Rene Lachemann,
would move 50 feet toward the outfield during his
at bats. Barry Larkin of the Reds—one of the top

Mark's strong arms and massive upper body let him drive balls that other hitters might pop up.

fielding shortstops in baseball—took refuge in shallow left field whenever Mark came to the plate. And anyone who dared to play Mark close usually paid the price. In a game against the Rockies, Mark turned on a pitch and produced a savage line drive that literally knocked Castilla on his rear end.

Needless to say, Cardinals' batting practice became baseball's most popular power display, as Mark would line ball after ball into the bleachers. Once, he hit 20 pitches out of the park! Normally, seats behind the dugouts or home plate are the most requested in a stadium. But when Mark and the Cardinals were in town, fans paid up to five times the normal price for the privilege of sitting in the left field stands. The chance of joining the mad scramble for a McGwire blast was worth it.

Going into the All-Star break, Mark had 37 home runs. Heading into August—traditionally his worst hitting month—he had upped his total to 45. Mark got through the month in fine shape,

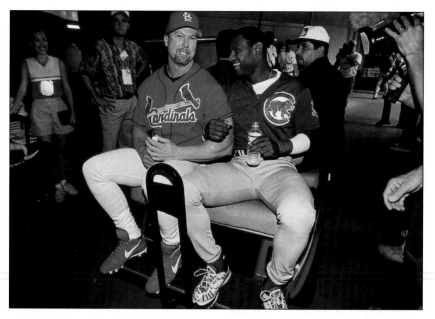

After a summer of chasing the home-run record together, Mark and Sammy are now close friends.

adding 10 more home runs. There now seemed to be no question that the all-time record would fall. The question was, who would break it? Sosa had kept pace with Mark throughout the summer, and the two players entered September knotted at 55.

Mark got to 61 first, on Sept. 7, when he launched his record-tying blast off Mike Morgan of the Cubs. In the stands sat the Maris family (Roger had died in 1985), and in right field stood Sosa, who was "stuck" on 58 home runs. Mark

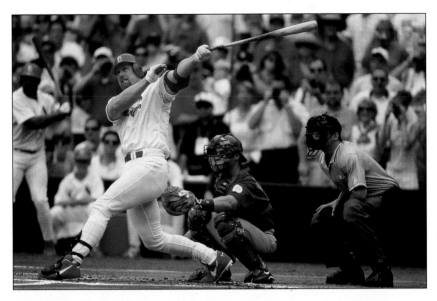

Mark launches his record-breaking homer against Steve Trachsel of the Cubs.

hugged the Marises, exchanged salutes with Sosa, and dedicated the home run to his father, who happened to be celebrating his birthday. The next night, Mark slugged number 62 off Chicago hurler Steve Trachsel. When his 340-foot line drive just cleared the fence, he jumped for joy— and actually missed first base as he started his home-run trot! When Mark planted his foot on home plate, he was met by the Cardinals' bat boy, Matthew McGwire. Mark picked up his son and acknowledged the roar of the crowd. "I was in shock," he remembers. "I was numb . . . I was just floating in space."

Mark was glad to put the home-run record behind him. But he did want to win the home-run title. Before he knew it, Sosa was on his tail again. In fact, the Chicago star actually passed Mark on Sept. 25, with his 66th four-bagger. Later that day, Mark blasted the equalizer, then added four more over the season's final weekend

to finish with an even 70. Sports fans around the country heard about Mark's final flurry on radio and television and could only shake their heads. Who could blame them? Even Mark finds his feat a little hard to

Mark and Matthew are reunited at home plate after his 62nd home run.

Mark acknowledges the cheers of the St. Louis fans.

Mark makes his final appearance of the year as a spectator at the 1998 World Series.

believe. "It's unheard of for somebody to hit 70 home runs," he says. "So I'm, like, in awe of myself right now."

How long will it take someone to break Mark's record? It seems impossible that anyone could approach 70 homers again, except Mark himself. The thought of going through another season like 1998, however, does not particularly appeal to him. Midway through '98, he actually had to stop watching television and reading newspapers to avoid thinking about the record. As Mark put it, he was "mentally exhausted."

Of course, from now on, every year Mark McGwire plays he will be expected to make a run at 71. And each time he fails to threaten his own record, a lot of people will be disappointed. That would have been an unpleasant prospect in years past, but he now knows how to deal with that kind of pressure. Whether he breaks his own record or comes up short, Mark will never forget what is really important in life and why he loves being a ball player. To him, no record is worth losing sight of those things.

C ⋆ H ⋆ R ⋆ O ⋆ N

1963 • Oct.1: Mark McGwire is born in Pomona, California.

1973 • Mark becomes a Little Leaguer at the age of 10. In his first at bat, he hits a home run.

1984 • Mark is named College Player of the Year at the University of Southern California.

• Mark is selected by the Oakland A's in the first round of the baseball draft and is also selected to play for Team USA in the 1984 Olympics.

1986 • Mark is called up to the majors when the minor-league season ends.

1987 • Mark breaks the home-run record for a rookie and is named American League Rookie of the Year.

O ✫ L ✫ O ✫ G ✫ Y

1989 • Mark and José Canseco lead the Oakland A's to the World Series championship against the San Francisco Giants.

1990 • Mark wins the Gold Glove for his excellent fielding.

1992 • Mark leads the American League with a .585 slugging average.

1996 • Mark leads the major leagues with a .730 slugging average and 52 home runs.

1997 • Mark moves to the National League when he is traded to the St. Louis Cardinals.

1998 • Mark establishes a major-league record with 70 home runs in a single season.

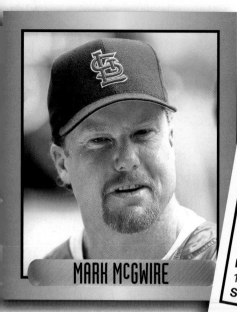

⭐ MAJOR LEAGUE STATISTICS ⭐

Year	Team	Runs	Home Runs	RBI	Batting Average
1987	Oakland A's	97	49	118	.289
1988	Oakland A's	87	32	99	.260
1989	Oakland A's	74	33	95	.231
1990	Oakland A's	87	39	108	.235
1991	Oakland A's	62	22	75	.201
1992	Oakland A's	87	42	104	.268
1993	Oakland A's	16	9	24	.333
1994	Oakland A's	26	9	25	.252
1995	Oakland A's	75	39	90	.274
1996	Oakland A's	104	52	113	.312
1997	Oakland A's	48	34	81	.284
	St. Louis Cardinals	38	24	42	.253
1998	St. Louis Cardinals	130	70	147	.299
Total		931	454	1121	.269

ABOUT THE AUTHOR

Mark Stewart grew up in New York City in the 1960s and 1970s—when the Mets, Jets, and Knicks all had championship teams. As a child, Mark read everything about sports he could lay his hands on. Today, he is one of the busiest sportswriters around. Since 1990, he has written close to 500 sports stories for kids, including profiles on more than 200 athletes, past and present. A graduate of Duke University, Mark served as senior editor of *Racquet,* a national tennis magazine, and was managing editor of *Super News*, a sporting-goods industry newspaper. His syndicated newspaper column, *Mark My Words*, is read by sports fans nationwide. He is the author of every Grolier All-Pro Biography and 17 titles in the Children's Press Sports Stars series.